Y0-GFM-691

WITHDRAWN

FOOD FUN

an easy-read ACTIVITY book

by Phyllis Hayes

Illustrated by
Irene Trivas

A GROLIER COMPANY
Franklin Watts
New York/London/Sydney/Toronto
1981

To Bill, Heather, Russell, and Mother

Library of Congress Cataloging in Publication Data

Hayes, Phyllis.
Food fun.

(An Easy-read activity book)
Summary: Includes simple recipes and craft activities using food, such as making a macaroni salad and using macaroni to make necklaces.
1. Cookery—Juvenile literature. [1. Cookery. 2. Handicraft] I. Trivas, Irene. II. Title. III. Series: Easy-read activity book.
TX652.5.H34 641.5 81-979
ISBN 0-531-04308-8 AACR2

Text copyright © 1981 by Phyllis Hayes
Illustrations copyright © 1981 by Irene Trivas
All rights reserved
Printed in the United States of America
6 5 4 3 2

CONTENTS

HAGAN MEMORIAL LIBRARY
CUMBERLAND COLLEGE
WILLIAMSBURG
7282505

Wherever a red star * appears, ask an adult to help you!

FOOD FUN is a collection of simple recipes and activities. Most of the time, you can use the same food that is in a recipe for part of an activity. You can do these things at home or at school with your friends.

Cooking and making things with food can be a lot of fun. But before you begin, ask a grown-up to read the directions with you. He or she knows that some knives are sharp, and that pots and pans get very hot on a stove. The grown-up will know how to help you best, so that you can really have FOOD FUN.

CHOCOLATE PUDDING IS FOR EATING

You need:

a measuring cup
a mixing bowl
2 cups (500 ml) cold milk
1 package instant chocolate pudding mix

1 large spoon

6 paper cups

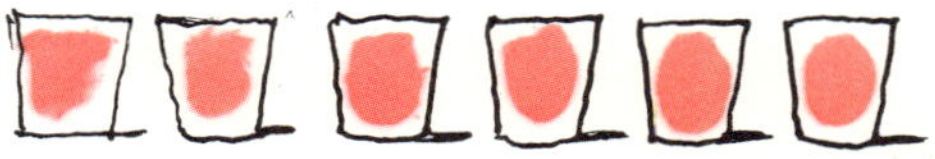

How to Do It:

1. Put the milk and the pudding mix into the bowl.

2. Stir quickly with the large spoon for two minutes.

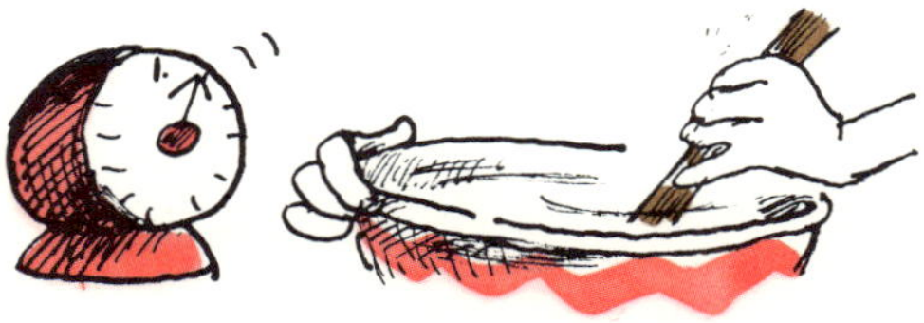

3. Spoon into six paper cups.

DON'T EAT ALL YOUR PUDDING.
TURN THE PAGE AND SEE HOW
YOU CAN MAKE A PUDDING PAINTING!

. . . AND FOR FINGER PAINTING

You need:
shelf or finger-paint paper
leftover chocolate pudding
hands or fingers

How to Do It:

1. Use the slippery side of either kind of paper.

2. Put two spoonfuls of pudding in the middle of the paper.

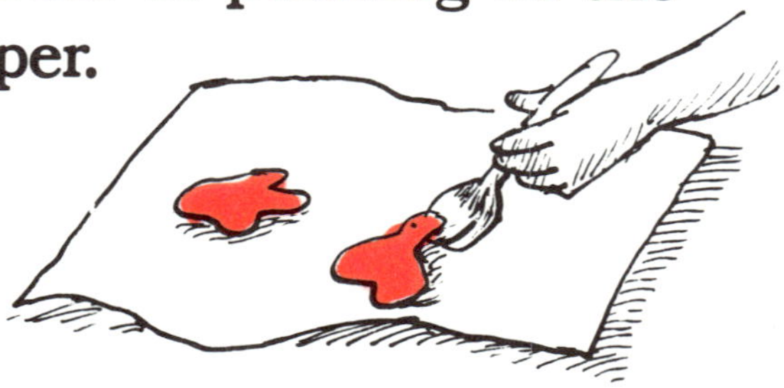

3. Paint with your fingers or hands. Make a picture of something you like! Be sure to cover all the paper.

4. Let your picture dry.

MARSHMALLOW FRUIT IS A DELICIOUS TREAT

You need:

a measuring cup

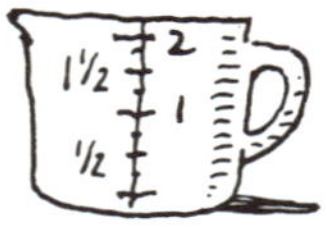

1 cup (227 g) small marshmallows
¾ cup (170 g) sour cream or yogurt

2 cups (454 g) drained canned fruit

a mixing bowl
a spoon

How to Do It:

1. Mix the marshmallows, sour cream or yogurt, and fruit together in the bowl.
2. Chill everything for several hours. Spoon into small serving dishes.

Why do elephants eat peanuts?

Because marshmallows get
stuck in their trunks!

MAKE A MARSHMALLOW MAN

You need:

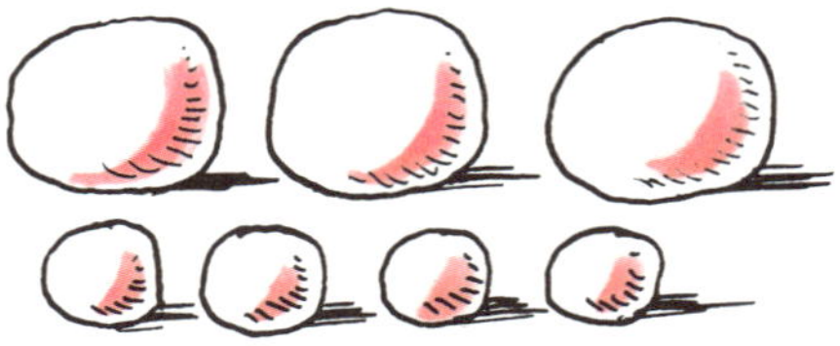

3 large marshmallows
4 small marshmallows
glue

a 2-inch (5 cm) circle cut from red or green felt

a toothpick

a black magic marker

needle and wool yarn

scissors

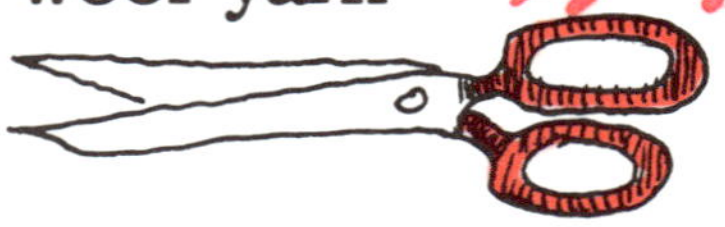

How to Do It:

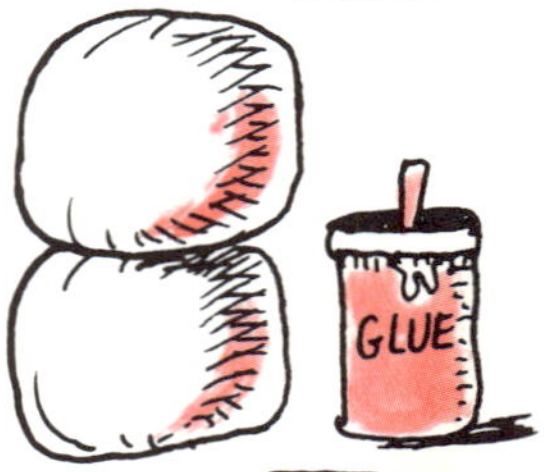

1. Glue two of the large marshmallows together to make the head and body.

2. Cut a 2-inch (5 cm) circle from the felt.

3. Glue the felt circle on top of the marshmallow head. This will be the brim of the hat.

4. Glue the last large marshmallow on top of the felt circle.

5. Carefully push the toothpick through the body.

6. Glue two small marshmallows on each side of the body, and two at the bottom, for arms and legs.

7. Let the marshmallow man dry for seven to ten days.

8. Use the marker to put on his face and buttons.

9. Thread the needle and sew through the hat to make a loop.

10. Tie the loop in a knot and hang on your Christmas tree. Or put the marshmallow man in a special place in your room! But don't eat him!

EASY-TO-MAKE BLENDER PEANUT BUTTER

You need:

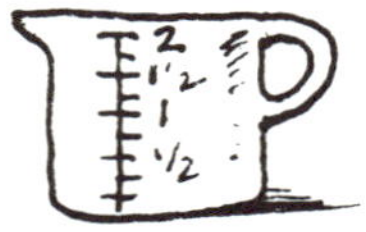

a measuring cup
1½ cups (340 g) salted, roasted peanuts
a blender
1 tablespoon peanut or vegetable oil

How to Do It:

* **1.** Put the peanuts in the blender and cover.
2. Process until it looks smooth.
3. Add the oil for creamy peanut butter.

How can you tell the difference between an elephant and a peanut?

Jump around on it!
If you don't get
any peanut butter,
it must be an elephant!

SAVE PEANUT BUTTER TO MAKE A TREAT FOR THE BIRDS

You need:
string
scissors
a pine cone

peanut butter
a table knife
birdseed
a shallow pan

How to Do It:

1. Tie a piece of string around the pointed end of the pine cone. Cut the string long enough so you can hang it from a tree branch.

2. Use the knife to spread the peanut butter over the pine cone.

3. Sprinkle the birdseed in the bottom of the pan. Then roll the pine cone in the birdseed.

4. Hang the pine cone bird-feeder on a tree. Watch the birds enjoy their treat!

MAKE GARDEN STEW WITH YOUR FRIENDS

You need:

a vegetable peeler
a knife
3 medium potatoes, each cut into 8 pieces
6 small carrots, cut into 1-inch (2.6 cm) pieces
1 large onion, cut into 6 pieces
1 cup (227 g) peas, sweet corn, or green beans
3 cups (750 ml) of water
3 beef stock cubes
3 ounces (85 g) or tube of tomato paste
a frying pan with a lid
a spoon
1 teaspoon salt
¼ teaspoon black pepper

How to Do It:

* **1.** Peel and chop the potatoes and carrots. Peel and slice the onion.

2. Put the water, stock cubes, and tomato paste into the frying pan. Do not cover.

* Turn heat to medium-high.

3. Stir until the cubes dissolve.

4. Add the vegetables, salt, and pepper. Stir again.

* **5.** When the stew starts to boil, put the lid on the frying pan and turn the temperature down.

6. Cook gently for 25 to 30 minutes.

SAVE THE CARROT TOPS!
Then turn the page and see why...

MAKE AN INDOOR CARROT GARDEN

You need:

a knife

the tops of the stew carrots

a shallow dish

water

How to Do It:

1. Cut the carrot tops about half an inch (1 cm) thick.
2. Put the carrot pieces in the shallow dish.
3. Add enough water to cover the bottom of the pan and part of the carrots.
4. Put in a sunny place indoors.
5. Keep adding water as needed.
6. The carrot tops will sprout in a few days.

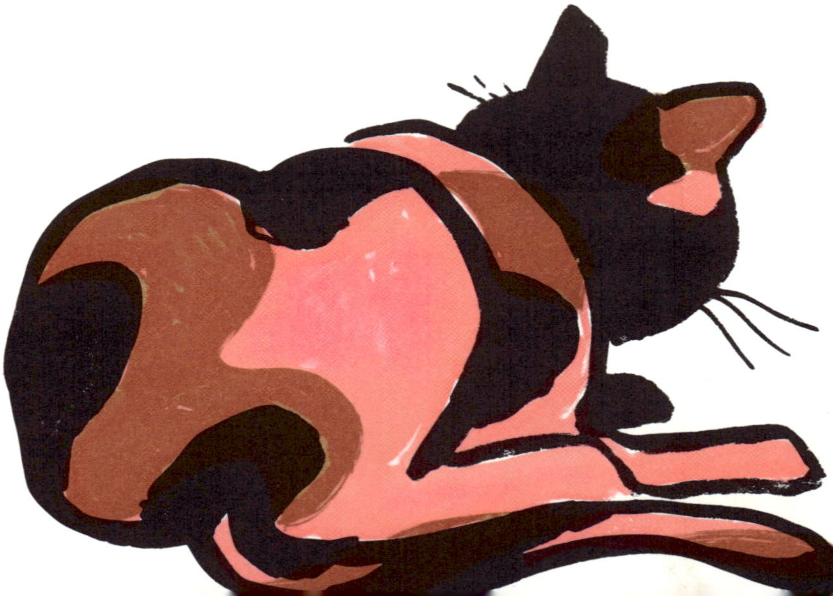

COOKED APPLES SMELL AND TASTE GOOD

You need:
4 cooking apples
a knife
a saucepan
water
¼ cup (57 g) of sugar
a sprinkle of cinnamon
a large spoon

How to Do It:

1. Wash and peel the apples.

*
2. Cut each apple into four pieces.

*
3. Cut away the core section. (This is the part that holds the seeds.)

*

4. Put the apples in the saucepan and add half an inch (1 cm) of water.

*

5. Cover the saucepan and simmer until the apples are tender.

6. Add sugar and stir.

7. Bring the apples to a boil.

8. Take the apples out of the saucepan with a large spoon.

9. Sprinkle with cinnamon and serve.

CAN YOU FIND A STAR INSIDE AN APPLE?

You need:
a large apple
a cutting board
a knife

How to Do It:

1. Put the apple on a cutting board.
2. Turn the apple so that the stem ends are not touching the board.
3. Cut the apple in half.
4. You will see a "star." This is what holds the five apple seeds.

MAKE STAR APPLE PRINTS

You need:

apple halves

a small knife

thick red tempera paint mixed in a shallow pan

paper towels

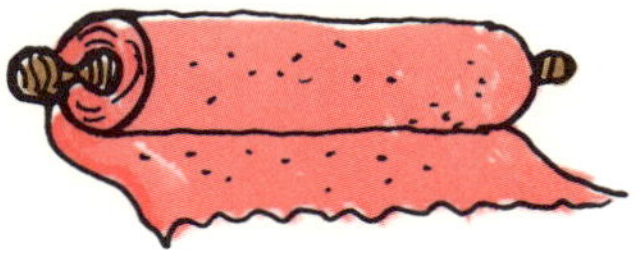

a piece of white paper

How to Do It:

1. Use the small knife and take out the seeds carefully.

2. Hold the sides of the apple in your hand and dip the apple in the paint.

3. Blot the apple once on a piece of paper towel. Then press the apple on the paper.

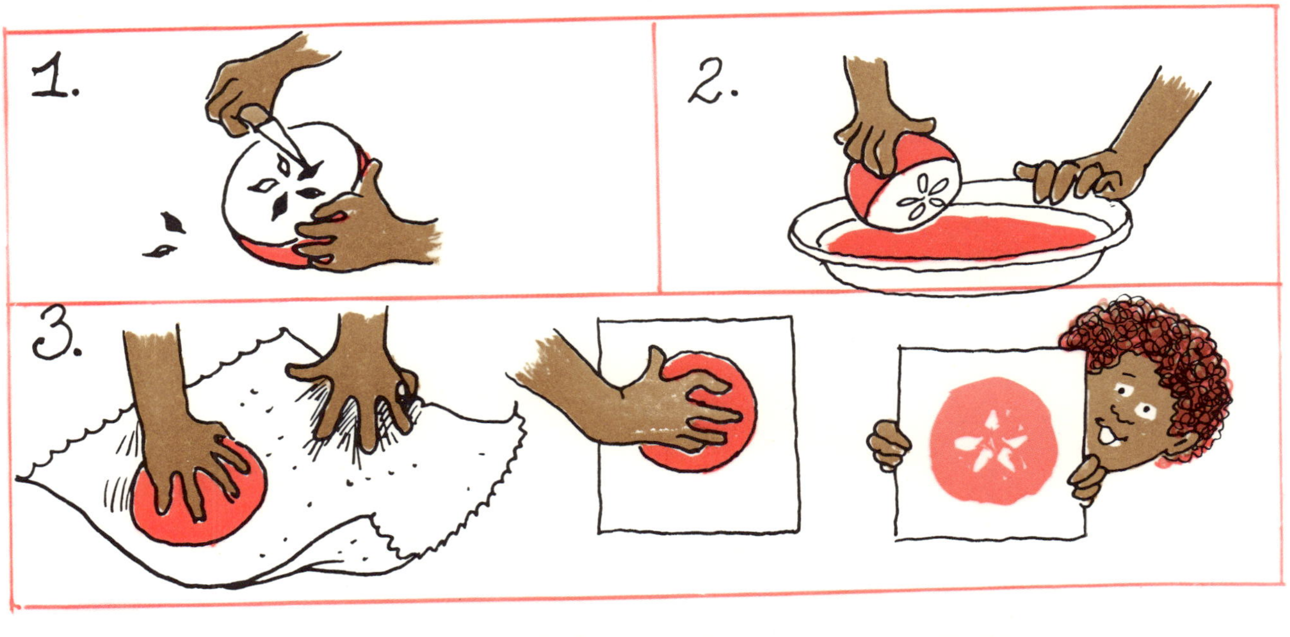

MAKE A SNIFF-AND-SMELL APPLE BALL

You need:
a ripe apple
toothpicks
whole cloves
an 8-inch (20 cm) square of nylon net
powdered cinnamon
ribbon

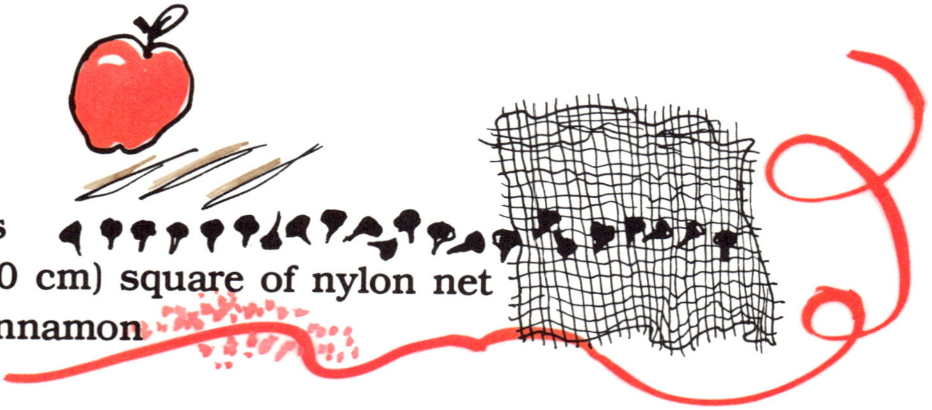

This is also called a pomander ball.

How to Do It:

1. Use the toothpicks to make holes all over the apple.

2. Push the cloves into all the holes until you can't see any more of the apple peel.

3. Put the apple on the net square.

4. Sprinkle cinnamon over the apple.

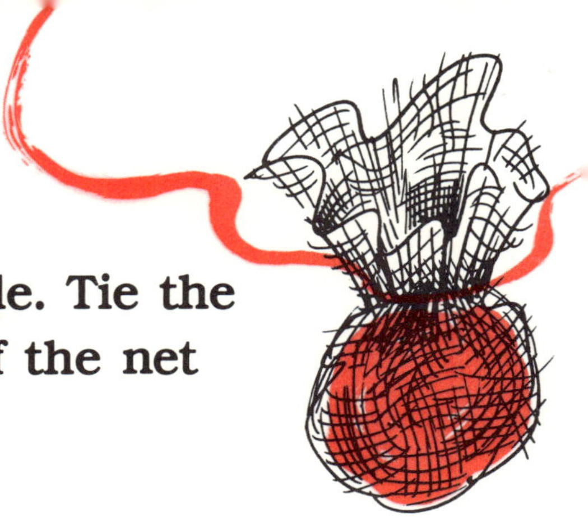

5. Gather the net around the apple. Tie the ribbon tightly around the ends of the net so the apple can't fall out.

6. Hang the ball to dry. Don't touch it for two or three weeks.

7. When the apple is dried, it will get smaller and begin to smell even better.

8. Hang your pomander ball in a closet. Or give it as a gift to a special friend.

CHOP A DELICIOUS MACARONI SALAD

Macaroni salad needs a lot of chopped vegetables. Ask some friends to help!

You need:

a large pot
6 cups (1500 ml) of water
8 ounces (227 g) of macaroni
a colander
a bowl
a knife
1 cup (227 g) chopped celery (about 3 stalks)
¼ cup (57 g) chopped green pepper
1 small chopped onion
¼ teaspoon black pepper
½ teaspoon salt
¼ cup (62.5 ml) mayonnaise
a spoon

How to Do It:

* **1.** Bring the water to a boil in a large pot.
2. Add the macaroni and boil for eight minutes.
* **3.** Put the colander in the sink. Pour the macaroni into the colander.

4. Rinse the macaroni with cold water. Drain thoroughly.

5. Put the macaroni in a bowl and add all the chopped foods, salt, and pepper.

6. Stir in the mayonnaise and mix well.

7. Eat the salad now or chill it in the refrigerator to eat later.

MACARONI IS ALSO FUN TO WEAR

You need:

different kinds of hollow macaroni, uncooked
string or cord
scissors
magic markers or paints

How to Do It:

1. Paint the macaroni or leave it plain. If you paint it, be sure to let it dry!

2. String the macaroni in any design you want by putting the string through the holes.

3. Make necklaces or bracelets by tying the two ends of the string into a knot.

EVERYONE LOVES LEMON LOLLIPOPS

To make 24 lollipops,

You need:

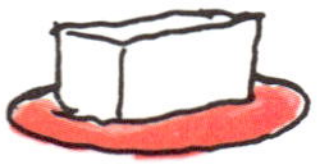

a baking sheet
½ stick (57 g) margarine

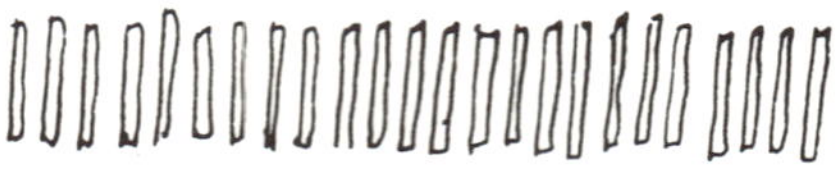

24 lollipop or popsicle sticks
a medium size pot

½ cup (125 ml) light corn (or golden) syrup

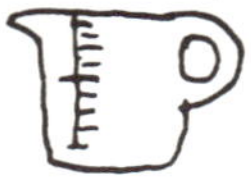

¾ cup (170 g) sugar
1 cup (250 ml) water

a candy (sugar) thermometer
a cup (250 ml) cold water

4 drops yellow food dye
4 drops lemon extract

a spoon

How to Do It:

1. Grease the baking sheet with a little extra margarine.

* **2.** Heat all the ingredients except the food dye and lemon extract. Bring to a boil.

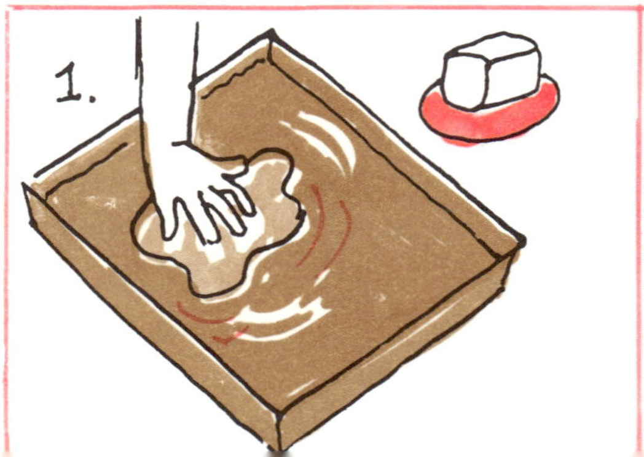

* **3.** Lower the heat. Cook at 270°F. on the thermometer until a teaspoon of syrup separates into hard threads when dropped in a cup of cold water.

4. Add the yellow food dye and lemon extract. Stir well.

5. Place the sticks on the baking sheet so they do not touch. Use a tablespoon to drop the syrup mixture over the top part of each stick.

6. Let cool before removing.

What happens when a cat
licks lemon lollipops?

It becomes a sour puss!

HAGAN MEMORIAL LIBRARY
CUMBERLAND COLLEGE
WILLIAMSBURG, KY. 40769